Strange Sheffield

Ghost Stories, UFO Sightings, and more...

Adrian Finney

Strange Britain

Copyright © 2021 Strange Britain

All rights reserved

Manuscript number: 091022

No part of this book may be reproduced, or stored in a retrieval system, or transmitted in any form or by any means, electronic, mechanical, photocopying, recording, or otherwise, without express written permission of the publisher.

Cover design by: Adrian Finney

Contact: strangebritainofficial@gmail.com

Follow "Strange Britain" on Facebook and Instagram

Special thanks to Natalie Tivey.

Without your encyclopedic knowledge of local Ghost Stories there really would be no book.

CONTENTS

Title Page

Copyright

Dedication

A warning…	1
Introduction	2
Barker's Pool - A Cautionary Tale from History	4
The Ghost Plane of Owler Bar	7
The Grey Lady of Graves Park & St James Church, Norton	9
The Black Dog of Bunting Nook	14
The Broken Neck Lovers	19
Charles Glover & Jack in Green	21
The Woodseats UFO Encounter of 1998	24
Cobner Woods	27
The Phantom Carriage of Graves Park	29
Spring Heeled Jack	31
The Out of Time Chip Shop of Firth Park	38

The Heroic Poltergeist of Mosborough	42
The Haunted Old People's Home	44
The Hand of Glory	47
Ecclesfield's Mysterious Red Flying V	51
The Soldier of Batemoor	53
The Stocksbridge Bypass	55
The Lizard's of Rivelin Valley	64
The Floating Feet of Angel Street	67
The Red Cloud of Woodthorpe	70
The Hound of Hillsborough	72
The Old Queen's Head	75
Vickers Corridor - Northern General Hospital	77
The Sheffield Incident	80
A Ghost on Fargate	96
Gabriel's Hounds	101
The Phantom Patrolman	103
Afterword	105

A WARNING...

This book contains tales of ghosts, UFOs, and of violent deaths and suicides.

Reader discretion is advised.

Sometimes names have been left out and dates have been left intentionally vague. This has been done to protect witnesses who either fear ridicule or, more often than not, wish to leave whatever it was they saw firmly in the past.

INTRODUCTION

Belief in ghosts and the paranormal is as old as humanity itself. Some of our oldest surviving texts speak of spectral visitors in the night.

It's clear that they are a part of our shared human experience.

A recent YouGov survey discovered that around a third of the population believe in ghosts, with another third open to the possibility, so it is a belief that is still very much with us today. And to take that one step further a full ten percent of the population believe that they have had actual, meaningful, contact with the other side.

A 2014 survey in trade magazine *Inside Housing* found almost 1,000 hauntings had been reported to local housing authorities. Both Cleeveleys and Kensington Councils spent taxpayer money on exorcism and blessing rituals. The cost of an exorcism, if you were wondering, is apparently just £60.

Their survey was comprehensive, pulling in data from over 500 social housing providers across the entire country, and it was one of the first to try and put a number to a situation that is often left as an anecdotal.

The big surprise was that almost two thirds of all reports, some 64%, came from terrified tenants here in Sheffield.

Some have said it's because Sheffield sits at a crossroads, a place where the barriers between worlds are at their thinnest, so it's a place where we can most easily catch a glimpse through to the other side.

Others think it might be because Sheffield City Council are a gullible lot so why not try it on with a ghost story?

Those that live here know the truth. Sheffield is one strange place that is built upon thousands of years of history.

If a place has been around this long it's bound to have picked up the odd ghost or two along the way.

The intention of this book is not to make sceptics into believers.

The interest is just to chronicle the tales of the weird and of the strange that our wonderful city has to offer.

BARKER'S POOL - A CAUTIONARY TALE FROM HISTORY

In late May 1875 a young apprentice, from a now long gone steel works, tragically lost his life in an accident. Back then deaths were still relatively commonplace in that industry but as this was a young and well respected lad there was a great outpouring of grief.

A funeral was held the next day and if this was a typically tragic story of the era that would have been that.

However just a few days later, in an upstairs window at the company's offices on what is now Barker's Pool, the glowing ghost of the young man was said to have been seen by a couple of passing witnesses.

The next night the glowing ghost appeared again. On the third night a crowd of several hundred turned up in the hope of seeing the ghost and, as if on queue, the figure once again appeared and was seen by the crowd for around five minutes. As the sun set the glowing figure vanished along with it.

On the fourth night things were getting out of hand. News of the ghost had spread like wildfire, thanks to word of mouth, and a crowd of several thousand had turned up hoping to see the ghostly figure. The local constabulary, fearing a riot, arrived and quickly took stock of the situation.

It was then, just before sunset, that the figure appeared yet again.

A quick thinking officer realised exactly what was happening and rushed into the offices speeding up the stairs two at a time.

By the time he reached the window the crowd outside was getting very rowdy, after all it's not every day you get to see a ghost, let alone get to see one four days in a row.

The officer had good reason to fear a riot. Back in 1873, not long after he joined the force, there was an alleged ghost sighting behind the newly opened train station. That incident resulted in a riot which saw over 2,000 people, mostly men and boys, running frenzied through the streets of Sheffield causing extensive property damage.

No one wanted a repeat of that.

The officer took a look out at the crowds outside and then he closed the window, and just like that the ghost vanished, only for it to reappear when he reopened the window.

The well trained officer had realised that the setting sun was causing a reflection to form on the open window, giving the illusion of a ghost, and it was this optical illusion that the crowd were witnessing.

He shouted this down, with a demonstration, to the crowd below, struggling to make himself heard over the baying mob. Once people realised what was happening the tension instantly broke. The crowd slowly dispersed and thankfully a potential riot was averted.

It's the rare ghost story that has an easy explanation, and it is even rarer to see in these historical stories, but it does go to show that when an obvious misidentification has occurred that there is always someone on hand to point it out.

The rest of the stories that follow might all have a simple, logical, explanation. But in many cases, despite there being multiple witnesses, no such easy explanation can be found.

THE GHOST PLANE OF OWLER BAR

Owler Bar, to the south west of Sheffield, is on the boundary between the city and the Peak District.

Overlooking much of Southern Sheffield it's a landscape that hasn't changed in centuries.

On certain November mornings a most unexpected sight can be seen in the skies overhead.

It was a World War 2 era RAF Dakota. The plane looks to be in trouble, with some witnesses reporting that the rear of the craft appears to be smothered with flames, as it flies low over the hills.

Witnesses are convinced the plane is about to crash and have raced over the brow of the hill expecting disaster. Instead? They're met with absolute nothing.

The plane, as impossible as it sounds, had vanished.

As anyone who has ever seen the Battle of Britain Memorial Flight, which features one of the last flying Dakotas, will know it is a very noisy plane.

You can hear the deep rumble of its engines approaching long before you see the plane.

However when this particular plane is witnessed? There is utter, total, silence.

A silence that's so jarring, given the low altitude of the plane, it's said to be unnerving. Unnatural even.

During the Second World War over four dozen planes crashed throughout the Peak District. In the region around the Dark Peak there is the twisted wreckage of one such plane, now rust eaten and almost unrecognisable, but still visible to this day. It's a haunting location to explore.

Given the amount of witnesses that have seen this plane over the years, it would appear that at least one of these lost aircraft has somehow found itself trapped in an endless loop, forever repeating its final moments before vanishing into the ether.

THE GREY LADY OF GRAVES PARK & ST JAMES CHURCH, NORTON

St James Church in Norton is a very old church, with a long history that dates back close to 1,000 years, and it is said to be the home to more than a few ghosts.

One of the more curious sightings in the church's record dates back to 1840.

The Parish Clerk and his apprentice were in the church practising on the organ. It was dusk, and the sun was setting outside, but they had good candles so were unphased by the dying natural light.

As the Clerk continued his playing the apprentice noticed that there was a woman sitting on one of the pews below. Seemingly she had come to listen to them play. But even from that distance he could tell that she was no ordinary woman. When the Clerk finished his piece the now panicking apprentice pointed out the woman on the pew below.

She was glowing softly, as if lit from within, and was ever so slightly translucent.

The Clerk, being a good and god fearing man who didn't have time for ghosts, thought that it must be a prankster so he decided to confront the woman.

He asked his apprentice to stay on the balcony, to ensure that she didn't run away, whilst the Clerk made his way down to the floor of the church below.

As he got to the end of the pew the woman, now fully transparent, simply faded away into nothing. All that she left behind was the faint smell of lavender.

He looked up at his apprentice on the balcony, seeing him white with fear, and it was then that the Clerks brain caught up with him and he began to process exactly what it was that they both had seen. With that both men screamed and fled the building.

Although they would return to the church both men vowed never again to play the organ for fear of conjuring up another spirit.

This was not to be the last sighting of this figure either. A grey, mist-like, figure of a woman has been seen a great many times around the church in the almost two centuries since this original sighting. It's especially during weddings that she likes to make her appearance known.

Her figure, perhaps drawn to the music, can be seen in more than a dozen wedding photos taken from the 1960s up to the 1990s. She's always located at the back of group shots, normally around the church's windows or doors, and she is always just transparent enough that you're never quite sure if she's really there or perhaps her figure is just a trick of the light.

The church isn't the only place this ghostly young woman has been seen. She's also been witnessed and photographed multiple times just a short walk away around the boating lake in Graves Park.

The artificial lakes in Graves Park, including the boating lake where she's often been witnessed, are all significantly older than the park itself. The lakes were originally built as a feature piece for the grounds of Norton House in the late 18th century.

Not long after their completion a young woman was sadly found floating lifeless in one of the lakes. She had drowned in somewhat mysterious circumstances and was dressed elegantly in a simple, flowing, grey dress.

She's said to still be seen there on occasion, floating over the water, looking mournful.

Her ghostly outline has also been captured on a great many photos taken in the park. Especially back when the lower lake was used as a boating lake.

Her ghostly floating figure can also often be seen in photos taken at night even to this day.

During a ghost walk at Halloween 2021, an event that was the genesis of the book you're now reading, we had half a dozen people capture unusual photos of an inexplicable mist over the waters that did resemble something of a female form.

It is believed that she is the same young woman that, back in 1840, scared the Clerk and his Apprentice in St James Church.

After researching local history it is now believed that the girl and her family were visiting Norton House, shortly after it's construction, and she was playing by the lake where she fell in and drowned after getting stuck amongst the lily pads.

Her father, distraught with grief and unable to deal with his loss, struck her existence from the record leaving us struggling to research her formal identity.

Of course there's also a much darker version of the story. Perhaps her father, upon finding out that she wasn't actually his daughter, killed her in a fit of rage before removing what he saw as evidence of his shame from the record.

Either way we think, given her apparent love of appearing in photographs, she simply doesn't want to be forgotten.

So if you ever find yourself around the lakes in Graves Park, especially at night, please let her know that she is very much not forgotten and then? Who knows. But perhaps, if you're lucky, she might just pose for a photograph.

THE BLACK DOG OF BUNTING NOOK

Bunting Nook, or Bunting's Nook as it was originally known, was named after local merchant Joseph Bunting.

He was a Sheffield man who, in the mid 18th century, left for America where he made his fortune selling Sheffield Steel to the colonies. When the American War of Independence broke out, with him being loyal to the crown and perhaps most importantly being loyal to his native Yorkshire, he decided to return to Sheffield bringing his now considerable wealth back with him.

Perhaps his most notable contribution to the area is that he was one of the men who originally founded the Bowls Club in Graves Park that still stands there to this day. The club, much like the boating lakes, predates the park itself by well over a century.

Despite us knowing who the road was named after we are still none the wiser as to why it was Bunting's Nook rather than, say, Bunting Street or Bunting Lane.

Bunting Nook has a history of ghost sightings that go back to the Middle Ages - long before it was ever known by its current name.

It's also a road that's known to be unusually quiet with local legend saying that it is a place where even the birds are afraid to sing- especially when there are spectres about. If you ever walk down Bunting Nook in the daytime you can hear for yourselves just how unnaturally quiet it is.

Perhaps the most well known, and most reported, of all the ghostly sightings is that of a huge ghostly black dog commonly referred to as Black Shuck.

Shucks are familiar beasts in English folklore, often appearing as unusually large black dogs, with huge saucer shaped glowing red eyes. A sizable number of sightings have even claimed that the Shuck has just one, huge, central eye with an iris of living fire.

The one spotted around Bunting Nook is said to resemble a large dog, similar in size to an Irish WolfHound, with glowing red eyes and a howl said to make your blood boil. Some reports even have the dog closer in size to that of a small horse.

The Shuck is said to appear suddenly in front of unsuspecting motorists, causing their engines to stall, but it is never the driver that the dog is after. Long before the era of the car he would jump out at passing carriages spooking them.

However, one thing that is consistent amongst all the sightings is that the Black Dog is always said to target passengers, leaving them terrified, and fearful for their lives.

There have even been a couple of instances where the driver hadn't even seen the dog. Their only indication that something was wrong was a total loss of power to their car as well as suddenly finding their front seat passenger screaming in fear.

Throughout the decades it's also worth pointing out that the Black Dog has exclusively targeted male passengers.

Almost all the sightings end with the Black Dog disappearing in a puff of black smoke accompanied by the distinctive smell of Sulphur.

Sightings of the Dog date back well over 300 years with the most recent encounter happening as recently as 2017.

The black dog is said to rise from one of the graves at St James Church, before padding his way towards and then along Bunting Nook, prowling the length of the road.

It's this that separates the black dog of Bunting Nook from other Black Shuck sightings from around the country.

Most are said to be the devil walking the earth

looking for souls to steal.

Not the one on Bunting Nook, in fact it is this author's belief that this Shuck isn't even a Shuck at all, he's actually most likely something called a Church Grim.

In old English folklore it was said that the first soul to be buried in a graveyard would be destined to remain bound there forever thus being left unable to move on.

The reason for this is that the first soul buried would automatically be assigned the role of Graveyard Protector. That soul would be eternally tasked with keeping the spirits of the dead at rest, with helping spirits to move on, and with keeping malicious spirits out.

As no one wanted to deny a human soul a place in heaven a dog was often sacrificed and buried under the cornerstone of an adjoining church.

The hope at the time being that the poor dog's ghost would become the graveyard's protector thus allowing any and all human souls that were to be buried there to move on.

Throughout the Middle Ages this was a surprisingly common practice, especially across Yorkshire, and there have even been a couple of archeological digs that have found the remains of some of these poor, unfortunate, dogs.

They kept us safe in this life and they're now keeping us safe in the next. There's even evidence to suggest that dogs might have been bred specifically for this purpose.

This, then, would have been the origin of the Black Dog of Bunting Nook.

A spirit forever tasked with protecting the graveyard at St James but also perhaps a spirit hell bent on trying to escape its fate, always making it along Bunting Nook but never any further, and perhaps seeking out the male descendants of those he believes responsible for his unjust death, those responsible for his having to spend an eternity without rest.

Or maybe its role is more typical to that of the Black Shuck of legend? Perhaps it only appears to those of a certain moral character and its intention is to scare them back on to a better path? The Black Dog does like to scare people, of that we have no doubt, but despite this there have been almost no reports of it actually causing any injuries, although he is a suspect in at least two deaths.

No one knows for sure.

All we do know is that if you're travelling alone down Bunting Nook it's one big, black, dog you definitely don't want to come across.

THE BROKEN NECK LOVERS

Of all the many ghosts said to haunt Bunting Nook perhaps the most tragic are the unfortunate pair now forever known as the Broken Neck Lovers.

They were a young couple, whose families were dead set against their relationship, so they decided to elope much like a local Romeo & Juliet.

But, much like Romeo & Juliet, this tale also ends in tragedy.

Whilst riding along Bunting Nook, escaping their families and I'm sure imagining a bright future together, they saw ahead of themselves the infamous Black Dog.

The giant dog's sudden appearance spooked their horse, thus causing both lovers to be thrown to the ground, and both of their necks snapped in the fall, killing them instantly.

It was two lives of promise and love cut tragically short in an instant.

They're said to wander the area to this day, with most sightings occurring just before sunrise, looking for a peace in death that they never found in their lives.

Be warned though. If you do see this pair of ghosts their heads are said to hang at an unnatural, grotesque, angle as a result of the injury that killed them.

It's also worth noting that, in the centuries of Shuck sightings, this is the only known fatality that he's alleged to have had his paw involved in.

CHARLES GLOVER & JACK IN GREEN

Despite Bunting Nook being a quiet little road, in a quiet part of the city, historically speaking Police Officers have often been said to avoid it if at all possible.

Why? Well every time an officer would walk along Bunting Nook they would find that they had stones thrown at them, had their helmets knocked off, and had their truncheons grabbed. Laughter was often heard and a green mist was said to hang in a roughly humanoid form.

The spirit responsible for these attacks is now known as Jack in Green, due to his appearing most frequently in the form of a green mist, but he wasn't always known by this name.

Charles Glover was a stable boy, and something of a prankster, who one day pulled one of his tricks on a local merchant.

The merchant, outraged at being the victim of such a childish prank, enlisted a group of local men to teach young Charles a lesson.

The group, perhaps flush with more than a little dutch courage, let things get tragically out of hand. Rather than scaring the young lad? They beat him up so severely that they accidentally killed him.

Those investigating his death put it down to a robbery that had gotten out of hand as, truth be told, no one mourned for poor Charles.

For most souls this could have led to eternal unrest and torment. But not our Charles. For him? It provided a whole new way to carry on his pranks, spooking passers by, attacking police officers, and generally causing himself a whole host of otherworldly mischief safe in the knowledge that he could no longer be caught.

Over the years there have been many sightings of a huge, hulking, green humanoid form said to emerge from a green mist in the dead of night. By all counts it looks almost like some kind of monster made from living plant matter.

Perhaps the most notable sighting of this was in 1958 when multiple police officers saw the figure emerge from the mist before walking along the road and disappearing back into a familiar green mist.

Although mostly sighted at night there have been a handful daytime sightings. In the now classic book *A Ghost Hunters Guide to Sheffield* it's reported that, one morning in the early 1980s, a couple saw the hulking green figure emerge on one side of the road, crossing it, before disappearing at the other side.

In the early 1970s there was even a sighting of a green police officer that was said to be skipping his way along Bunting Nook before disappearing in a green mist. This sighting was allegedly witnessed by several police officers.

One thing has become very clear - the spirit of Charles Glover, now known as Jack in Green, is still there to this day and it's obvious he's learnt more than a few tricks since his passing. If whatever you're seeing on Bunting Nook starts or ends in a green mist, no matter what shape it may take between, you too have been a victim of one of his undead pranks.

For those wishing to pay their respects Charles Glover's grave can be found in the far wall of the graveyard at St James' Church Norton.

His headstone reads:

Sacred to the Memory of Charles, son of Charles and Hannah Glover of Holmhirst, who departed this life on July 5th 1846 aged 16

In Evil hour I fell, oppressed with pain by bloody minded men untimely slain.

O May they find, through Jesus crucified, that mercy their evil hands to me denied

THE WOODSEATS UFO ENCOUNTER OF 1998

Not all the strange occurrences around Sheffield are ghostly in their origin. Some might be, quite literally, out of this world.

In January 1988 two officers serving at Woodseats Police Station, Inspector David Tingle and DS Chris Thomson, reported a sighting of a strange shaped craft in the sky hovering low overhead. After thirty seconds or so it shot off, apparently heading straight up, and within a few seconds it was gone.

Their report was passed on to the MOD who designated it as unexplained.

Several such sightings have been made since then in the skies above Woodseats.

In early May 1998 one of the strangest UFO sightings in modern history was witnessed in the skies above. It is said that hundreds of members of the public, along with over a dozen police officers dotted throughout the area, all saw a weird orange blob like object fly across the valley heading towards

Graves Park, where people lost sight of it.

What makes this one exceptionally unusual in UFO circles is that there was also a witness who saw the object from the air. A small aircraft was seen by many to fly directly OVER the unusual object. The police managed to track down the pilot and were able to speak with him. He described it as glowing orange and said that it looked to be organic, as to him it appeared almost like a flying jellyfish, and that from his vantage point it appeared to have been about double the size of his small plane.

All the police officers involved filed reports with the Ministry of Defence and with the Civil Aviation Authority. However in the FOIA report that was obtained all their badge numbers were redacted and the officers were supposedly ordered never to speak of the incident again.

A few years ago the MOD released almost all of their UFO files, they're now available to view in the National Archive, but curiously this incident wasn't amongst the released documents.

What's the truth here? Aliens? Ghosts? A large piece of orange fabric blowing in the wind? Who knows. Some people have even hypothesised that the area is a weak point between realities so whatever it was that people saw? It could have an inter dimensional interloper.

One thing we do know for sure is that a couple

of weeks later the object, whatever it was, had returned. At close to midnight on May 31st 1998 the glowing orange blob was back and seen by 4 police officers for around 15 minutes. It was manoeuvring slowly overhead and through the use of binoculars they worked out that what was seen was definitely a real object, rather than a trick of the light or an optical illusion, but beyond that they were at a loss.

What makes this one interesting is that we do actually have the log number for it:

Police log 1249 of 31/05/1998.

The log states that video was taken of the object, from multiple different locations, and that the video was later seized by the MOD never to be seen again.

What was the object?

To quote a popular show of the time?

The Truth is Out There

COBNER WOODS

One of the oldest surviving pieces of woodland in Sheffield, and perhaps the whole country, is the small woods at the top of Cobner Road.

The woods are there on the very earliest surviving maps of the area and they have been left untouched ever since. It's almost as if people instinctively knew to leave them be as there is something lurking inside them.

Throughout the centuries there have been reports of shadowy figures prowling and whispering, always just at the edge of peoples vision, but definitely there. Watching. The most commonly reported sighting is that of a figure said to resemble a man with a bear's head.

On certain moonless nights white glowing figures are also said to be seen dancing in the woods.

No one is sure of the origins, there have been sightings for as long as there have been people living in the area, only that whatever lurks in that little piece of woodland is far older, and perhaps stranger, than we can possibly imagine.

It's interesting how little the sightings have changed over the centuries. Be they 17th or 21st century the figures seen are consistently described.

Perhaps you've seen them too?

THE PHANTOM CARRIAGE OF GRAVES PARK

Graves Park is the biggest park in Sheffield and is enjoyed by thousands of visitors every year but for this book? It's those ghostly visitors we are most interested in.

On cold and frosty nights an old horse drawn carriage can sometimes be seen and heard thundering through the park.

But this is no ordinary horse drawn carriage. There is no visible driver, there are no visible passengers, and perhaps strangest of all? The carriage is said to hurtle through flying a full foot above the ground.

The carriage appears on the path near the cafe, then rushing down towards the old boating lake and fish ponds, before finally veering off towards Norton House where it is said to screech to a halt.

On the very coldest of nights the phantom horse's hoof prints can even be seen on the ground, despite the carriage said to be flying above, whereas on other nights it can only be heard rather than seen.

No one knows when it was first sighted, the earliest reports predate Graves Park itself by decades, nor does anyone know who it is that might be travelling inside the carriage.

Speculation ranges from a distraught parent of one of the two sadly deceased lovers on Bunting Nook all the way through to Florence Nightingale, given Norton House's past as a hospital, although this feels more like wishful thinking given the carriage started appearing decades before the House became a hospital.

All we know is that on the coldest of nights, if you're feeling particularly brave or perhaps foolhardy, you can head into Graves Park and, if the moon is right, you too might just catch a glimpse of The Phantom Carriage of Graves Park.

SPRING HEELED JACK

The imposing figure of Spring Heeled Jack is one with a long history in British folklore.

Often said to be an impossibly tall man, with burning red eyes, a long flowing cape, and a top hat. The most unusual aspect of his, the one that was to give him his name, was his ability to jump impossibly huge distances and to climb seemingly unclimbable walls.

He would often be found peeping through windows before leaping across rooftops letting out a maniacal cackling laugh.

He was first spotted back in 1840 when he began terrorising the Whitechapel area of London. By the end of that decade sightings of him had spread across much of the U.K.

However it wasn't until the late 1860s that Jack had made his way up to Sheffield. Sightings, matching those earlier ones in Whitechapel, were initially made around the Heeley area. The Midland Railway was coming to town, with Sheffield and Heeley stations both opening in 1870, and it looks like Jack came along for the ride.

The initial clutch of sightings were all on Chesterfield Road in an area centred around the railway bridge and the old Heeley station. All the witnesses claim to have seen a tall thin figure, with glowing red eyes, who leapt impossible distances as he bound across the rooftops.

By 1871 Jack had made his first appearance in Attercliffe. The sightings again matched those initial reports from Whitechapel back in the 1840s and from Heeley just a couple of years earlier.

He was said to be banging on doors and windows, peering in, and then laughing maniacally as he jumped away across the rooftops.

By the 1880s reports across the country were starting to wane. The last recorded sighting in Whitechapel, the place where Jack first thrust himself out on to the world, happened just a couple of days before another Jack was to appear on the scene.

That other Jack? He was the infamous serial killer Jack the Ripper, who began his horrific murder spree on a Whitechapel already terrified by his Spring Heeled namesake, and would eventually become a name even more widely known and feared than Spring Heeled Jack ever had been.

Within a few years Spring Heeled Jack was remembered as nothing more than an urban legend.

Many assumed that would be that for Spring Heeled Jack but the world hadn't yet seen the last of him.

In the early 1920s the people of Attercliffe were woken by the sound of someone, or possibly something, racing across their rooftops. On groggily looking out of their windows they saw a figure, one who perfectly fit the description of Spring Heeled Jack, jumping effortlessly from rooftops on one side of the street to rooftops on the other.

The residents, now suddenly very much awake, watched in fear as Jack leapt while his maniacal laughter filled the air.

The police were summoned but, aside from damage to the rooftops that would have been consistent with a heavy man running around on top of it, nothing more was found and, after a half dozen more sightings over the next two weeks, Jack was once again gone.

Twenty years later Sheffield found itself under a very different kind of attack. The Sheffield Blitz was underway which saw German Bombers targeting the city's many steel works, destroying large parts of the city in the process, and killing hundreds if not thousands of innocent people.

In the midst of all this chaos and tragedy Spring Heeled Jack chose to make his return. This time round he was once again seen exclusively around Heeley where he was running up and down the rooftops on Chesterfield Road cackling his manic laugh, a laugh so loud that it rang out above the sounds of the falling bombs.

By 1945 the sightings had again ceased and many thought, once again, that was that.

Then, in the late 1970s, Jack was back only this time he was more active than ever. He also had acquired a new nickname:

The Prowler.

The Prowler, as many Attercliffe locals had taken to calling him, was leaping from rooftop to rooftop, leering into windows, and terrifying the poor residents like you wouldn't believe.

Then, at Christmas 1978, things escalated to a much more destructive level. Back then the area around what is now Sheffield Arena, where all the sightings were centred, was still old Victorian back to back housing. It was, in fact, the last of Sheffield's infamous Victorian slum housing. There were also several factories dotted about the area.

One of these factories had 3 large chimneys and it was that Christmas when residents of the area were woken by an almighty crash. Something, or someone, has somehow managed to knock the top 20ft or so off of all three chimneys.

The initial belief was that an aircraft must have clipped the top of the chimneys. It was the only logical explanation. However no damaged or downed aircraft could be found.

The police quickly arrived on the scene and a figure, matching the description of Spring Heeled Jack, was seen as his distinct cackle rang out. A foot chase ensued with the police cornering the figure in a dead end.

It was then, in front of over half a dozen officers, that Spring Heeled Jack made his escape. He ran straight up a sheer vertical wall, some 4 stories high, leaving the police dumb struck. And all that they could hear was the sound of his laughter echoing out into the night sky.

The police officers involved were all taken in for a debriefing and were told, in no uncertain terms, that they were to forget what they saw. Mythical monsters couldn't possibly be on the prowl in 1970s Sheffield.

Perhaps it might be for the best if they were to stop drinking whilst on duty?

Of course that didn't work. The Prowler was still at large and local residents were in a panic.

Spring Heeled Jack then upped his game. He began appearing all across the city, from Attercliffe to Heeley to Broomhall, seemingly at random. And the police were at a loss as to what exactly was going on.

By the Christmas of 1980 it was decided enough was

enough. A large-scale operation was discreetly put into place that would essentially see every available officer sent out on patrol with the hope that they'd catch The Prower. Of course they didn't believe him to be a supernatural monster, so they refused point blank to call him Springheeled Jack, instead they thought that it was all an elaborate hoax. One that they were hellbent on catching the perpetrators of.

But little did they know that Jack had already been sighted for the last time. It would be an altogether different, and truly evil, monster that they were about to bring to justice.

On January 2nd 1981 South Yorkshire police stumbled across the notorious serial killer Peter Sutcliffe aka The Yorkshire Ripper.

It was his first night hunting in Sheffield, and he almost had a victim here, but thankfully the hunt for The Prowler meant that there were more than enough officers on patrol that fateful night. Sutcliffe was initially arrested for having a broken light on his car before the police realised exactly who it was that they had sitting in their cells thus ending his reign of terror.

As for Spring Heeled Jack? He hasn't been seen since. It's a very curious parallel to what happened back in the late 1880s with Jack the Ripper - both serial killers were active against the backdrop of multiple Spring Heeled Jack sightings.

Perhaps Jack is an evil spirit that was leading these wicked men to commit their wicked acts?

Or perhaps, just perhaps, he's there as a warning. His sightings act as a reminder for us to always be on guard and that danger is always just around the corner.

He's showing us that we need to be aware that there are some truly evil, all too human, monsters in our midst.

THE OUT OF TIME CHIP SHOP OF FIRTH PARK

Strange sightings in Sheffield aren't limited to ghosts and UFOs. Sometimes things can be a whole lot *weirder* than that.

In 1990 a mother and her daughter were heading home through Firth Park carrying multiple bags of shopping. They got off their bus and began the short walk home.

It was late in the year, so already dark, when they spotted something that they were sure wasn't there the day before.

It was a Chip Shop, the lights were on, and they could see people inside. It looked old fashioned but very inviting.

As they only lived around the corner they decided to drop their heavy bags off at home and then head back for some now much wanted fish and chips.

When they returned to the shops, just a couple of minutes later, the chip shop was nowhere to be found. Instead, on the spot where they were certain that they had spotted the inviting chippy, was a small hardware store.

Confused, they retraced their steps back to the bus stop in case they were mistaken, but it quickly became clear that they weren't.

As they got back to the hardware shop they asked the owner, who was now locking up outside, if he knew of any local chip shops. The owner, with a knowing look on his face, turned to them and said *"You've seen it haven't you?"*

He then revealed that, back in the 1950s, his shop had indeed once been a chip shop but that it had burned down at some point in the early 1960s. His shop now occupied what was both the chippy and the small newsagents that was originally next door.

The mother and daughter were dumbfounded.

What was it that they had seen? Could it have been a spectral manifestation of a long gone shop? Or perhaps something altogether more weird was at play.

Time slips, whilst not unknown, are still a very rare phenomenon. Perhaps something happened that winter's evening that allowed them a literal glimpse into the past?

Further investigation shows that this mysterious, out of time, chip shop has been sighted at least a dozen times since.

In one instance a man actually went inside to order himself some tea. He ended up being chased out for allegedly trying to pass off fake money.

This happened at the end of the 1990s, with the man in question paying in modern decimalised money, but we have to remember that back when the chip shop was open we were still using pounds, shilling, and pence. So his modern £5 note would have looked very fake indeed to those inside the chippy not familiar with modern currency.

The man left the shop and upon leaving he felt a sensation like static electricity on the back of his neck. He turned around to see he had actually just exited the existing hardware store. But he was certain that it was the chip shop he had left...

Scared he did the only sensible thing he could think of. He headed for the closest pub he could find and he ordered himself a stiff drink.

Sightings of the chip shop still occur every now and again.

Perhaps, like a great many ghostly goings on, sightings are actually happening all the time. It's just that most people passing by are completely oblivious to how truly strange the sight before them actually is.

If you passed a chip shop in a car or whilst riding on

a bus would you give it a second glance?

THE HEROIC POLTERGEIST OF MOSBOROUGH

It's a widely held misbelief that hauntings are always malicious. The simple truth is that most hauntings are actually benign in their nature.

There was a house on School Street, in Mosborough, that once found itself with a poltergeist.

It was the early 1980s when little things began to happen. It would start with small items moving on their own, a child's laughter coming from the empty loft, along with other low level activity.

Over the coming months the family living there, amused by their supernatural trickster, came to see him (for they were sure it was a young boy) as part of the family.

That Christmas they even got a Christmas card for the ghost and addressed it to "he who bumps in the night."

To them he was a friendly, reassuring, presence.

Easter 1982 was when things changed dramatically. The family were rudely awoken by their beds being slammed up and down, the whole house was shaking, and it felt like an earthquake. One of their beds was said to be floating above the ground.

Wondering what the hell was going on, and why their formally friendly poltergeist had changed so suddenly, the family realised that they could smell burning.

There was a fire downstairs and it was quickly starting to spread.

The family, now fearing for their lives, quickly realised that their friendly poltergeist had actually been trying to wake them to warn them.

It was only thanks to the ghosts' actions that the family made it out alive.

The fire brigade came quickly, and thankfully most of the house was saved, so it was only a few months before the family were able to return.

Sadly they returned to find the house empty.

The fathers theory was that their friendly poltergeist had used up all of his energy to wake the family, saving their lives, but sacrificing his own afterlife in the process.

THE HAUNTED OLD PEOPLE'S HOME

There is a well known old people's home in the Dore area of Sheffield where the residents often receive some unexpected visitors.

Most of the time the residents live in peace and comfort. But at meal times it can sometimes be an entirely different story.

Some residents have been said to become distressed saying that they don't want to *"look at the children."*

It reached a point where a second, separate, dining room had to be set up for those who said that they did not want to see the children.

Looking into the building's history we find a possible explanation. It was originally built in the early 1900s as a home for ill children. It carried on in this role until the 1950s, when its patients were transferred to the local Children's Hospital, and the building was repurposed to its current use - an old people's home.

The current dining room was the same room that had once housed the ward for terminally ill children. And based on the evidence we have it would appear that a few of them have chosen to stay around to this day.

It is said that those who see the children are those who are closest to death although it has to be said that this claim hasn't been substantiated. It does raise some curious thoughts though.

Could they be there to welcome dying residents over to the other side?

The children aren't the only ghosts to haunt the home. Staff have often seen the shadow of a man hanging off of the main staircase.

One of the first managers of the home, back when it was used for ill children, had hung himself there. He left no suicide note so it's a mystery as to why he had taken his own life.

It was suggested at the time that perhaps the constant sadness of his surroundings had taken the ultimate toll on him.

Perhaps what's at play could be the stone tape theory? This suggests that, by means as yet unknown, surrounds can somehow record an imprint of previous events. This can then replay and thus explain hauntings.

ADRIAN FINNEY

When a building such as this has had such a deep history of death and sadness, perhaps it has left an impression, one some are more capable of seeing than others?

THE HAND OF GLORY

There are few artefacts in folklore as curious, or as grisly, as The Hand of Glory.

To make a Hand of Glory you first need a hand. Not just any old hand will do. It must be the severed hand of a murderer and more specifically? It must be the hand that committed the wicked deed.

Next the hand must be mounted, wrist down and fingers up, on a plinth. Finally each finger must be topped with a candle of finest wax.

Now, if you've followed all of these steps, you'll have yourself a Hand of Glory that's ready to use.

Why would you go through the trouble of all of these steps? Well once all of the candles are lit it is said that all who are asleep in The Hand's vicinity will remain unconscious until the flames are extinguished by goat's milk. Any other liquid would trap those affected permanently in a coma-like state.

This makes them incredibly useful tools for burglary and robbery.

A long gone Inn, just outside of Sheffield, was the location for one of the few recorded cases of A Hand ever being used.

On the Moors to the south of Sheffield, heading out towards Bakewell, was a successful inn. Being on a busy trading route it's nightly turn over made it an attractive and tempting target to those with ill intent.

A trio of thieves had been frequenting the inn, planning their robbery, when one of the men found himself on the wrong side of the law. A bar fight had seen him kill a fellow drinker. This happened in Sheffield and he was hung outside the Noose and Gibbet pub in Attercliffe.

The two men went to collect their friend's body, after it had been left hanging for two weeks, and then they realised that his body had a perfectly good hand so why not lop it off and make themselves a Hand of Glory?

With the hand safely detached, and their friend's decaying corpse now floating off serenely down the River Don, the two men headed out to Owler Bar.

It was the dead of night when they arrived outside the inn. Making sure everyone inside was asleep, as best as they could, they proceeded to light the Hand of Glory.

To test the Hand's powers they first shook a man

slumbering just outside the pub and he did not wake.

Feeling emboldened by this they forced the lock and went inside, excited by the prospect of stealing what to them would have been a life changing amount of money, but unfortunately this excitement, much like the life of one of the two men, was to be short lived.

The Landlord had woken up, stirred by the noise of the door being broken into, and he quickly went for his gun. He shot one of the men, killing him instantly, whilst the other surrendered.

The man was shaking, rocking back and forth, muttering that it hadn't worked. Why hadn't it worked?

It was daylight when the local Sheriff arrived and found that the surviving robber had quite the tale to tell.

It turns out that they'd made one crucial mistake when assembling their Hand of Glory.

Their friend was left handed and it was that hand he used whilst committing murder. The two thieves, in their drunken stupor, hadn't realised this and had made off with his right hand.

What happened to the surviving robber, after his confession, we don't know.

But given that there haven't been any further reports surrounding attempted uses of a Hand of Glory we hope that he gave up his life of crime.

ECCLESFIELD'S MYSTERIOUS RED FLYING V

It was late February back in 1988 and PC Susan Jackson's patrol had been pretty run of the mill when a call came in over her radio. Apparently there had been reports of strange lights seen in the skies above.

She pulled her patrol car over and looked to the south and, much to her surprise, there was indeed something in the sky. She had no idea what it was but she described it as a large, V shaped object, that was covered in rows and rows of red pulsing lights.

She'd left the engine running on her police car but could still hear a whirring / whooshing noise coming from the object as it slowly made its way towards her before passing by directly overhead.

Whatever it was it wasn't doing much more than walking speed which, to her, defied all logic.

She got back on her radio and asked if there were any

other officers in the area. Luckily enough another officer was only about a mile away in the direction the object was headed.

He also saw the object and said that when it passed directly over his position it appeared to stop and hover for around 30 seconds.

The switchboard at police headquarters was now getting several dozen calls all concerning this strange, flying, object.

As the officer watched the object it started accelerating away before he lost sight of it as it headed off towards Grenoside.

Four other police officers all saw the same object from different vantage points across the area and all of them gave identical descriptions.

Whatever was seen that night was a textbook book definition of a UFO. It was an object, it was flying over North Sheffield, and crucially? It still remains very much unidentified.

THE SOLDIER OF BATEMOOR

On certain nights, when the wind is still and the sky is clear, an otherworldly sight can be seen marching proudly across Batemoor Park.

That sight is a World War One era soldier, marching rifle in his hand, on his never ending patrol.

Knowing the history of the area, and plotting a map of his sightings, it's clear that he's patrolling the perimeter of the now long forgotten RAC (Royal Air Corps) Norton.

During the First World War RAC Norton was a very important base. Not only did it house and service reconnaissance planes, a then cutting edge technology, it was also home to several thousand German POWs.

He was said to have been a soldier patrolling the base and that somehow he had fallen into a quarry, located roughly where Batemoor Park is now, and had sadly died as a result. He's now stuck, having to spend his eternity trying to finish his patrol, and to get back to his barracks.

However there is something strangely reassuring about his presence, knowing that there is still a soldier on patrol, still keeping us safe from the other side.

THE STOCKSBRIDGE BYPASS

When a road officially opens on Friday 13th you know that there is bound to be something strange about it and that's certainly true of the Stocksbridge Bypass which formally opened to traffic on Friday 13th May 1988.

At just 5 miles long the bypass connects Sheffield with the Peak District and Snake Pass on to Manchester, yet despite appearing to be a fairly ordinary stretch of road, it saw over 14 fatal accidents within its first 10 years of being open and even to this day it still sees an unusually high number of accidents along its short length.

But this is no ordinary stretch of road. It's arguably the most haunted road in the whole of England. And it's reputation was cemented nationally long before the road was even completed,

On the night of September 11th 1987 two security guards were on duty. The road's construction was well underway but parts of it were still very much a building site.

They initially heard what they assumed to be a group of children laughing and singing. They checked their watches and it was just after midnight.

Fearing that at best a group of local children were playing on the unsafe site, and at worst that they were perhaps young vandals up to no good, they picked up their torches to investigate.

From a distance they could see a group of children, somewhere between eight and ten of them, dancing around a large electricity pylon as though it was some kind of Maypole. It was a most unusual sight given the lateness of the hour and the fact that it was some distance to the closest house.

They decided to confront the children so got in their Land Rover to drive around and up to the Pylon. Once they got closer they noticed that the children were wearing unusual clothing. They described them by saying that it looked like they had on mediaeval or perhaps Victorian era clothing.

Wondering what was going on the two security guards got out of their car for a closer look. It was at that precise moment when the Children promptly vanished before their eyes, with them fading away in a matter of seconds, but their laughter could still be heard faintly on the breeze.

Confused, rather than afraid, the two security guards were left wondering what they had just witnessed? It was at that point that they noticed an intimidating hooded figure was watching them from the vantage point of Pea Royd Bridge.

The security guards decided to split up. One man would remain where he was whilst the other took their car up to the bridge to get a better look. Fast thinking that they were the victims of some kind of practical joke they thought that they'd be able to catch any trickster in the act.

Once the car got to the bridge and shone its lights at the figure it quickly became clear that what was going on was not a practical joke at all. Instead it was actually something else entirely.

Something supernatural.

The car's headlights shone straight *through* the figure as though he wasn't there. The illumination did however help them to see his dark, featureless face, and showed that he was, in fact, hovering several feet above the ground.

The two men quickly returned to their office and, not knowing what else to do or who else to call, they headed straight to the local police station. PC Dick Ellis was the man who met the two security guards and it is fair to say he was sceptical. He told the men that ghost sightings were very much outside of the police's area of interest.

Perhaps they'd be better off calling a Priest?

A couple of hours later the Rector of a local church rang the police and was put through to PC Ellis. He told him that he had the two men sitting in his office and they were refusing to leave. They clearly had been scared to their core by their encounter.

The following night PC Ellis, along with his partner PC Beat, decided to drive up to investigate.

Initially they spotted something moving on the bridge. A quick investigation showed it to be nothing more than a loose sheet of plastic. Securing it with a couple of bricks the two officers got back into their car laughing. Who'd have imagined two seasoned security guards could have gotten so spooked by plastic blowing in the wind?

Deciding to call the investigation off PC Ellis reached for his seat belt when he saw something that shocked him to his core. A hooded, partially transparent, figure was just outside of his window. He yelled in fright and the figure disappeared before instantly appearing on the other side of the car frightening PC Beat.

The two police men decided that this would be a very good time to make their exit but they found that their patrol car just wouldn't start. After several minutes of the hooded figure ominously circling the car, appearing and disappearing in the blink of an eye, their engine finally spluttered into life.

All throughout the hasty drive back to the police

station there were sounds coming from the boot of their car. It was as though someone, or maybe something, was trapped inside. Pulling over they cautiously opened the boot only to find it empty.

They entered the incident into their log and it was this single act that firmly cemented the reputation of the Stocksbridge Bypass into international legend.

The local newspaper, The Sheffield Star, regularly read through the logs on the lookout for stories. They'd never seen a lot quite like this one before so it quickly became front page news.

From there the story grew and grew and soon the whole world was reading about what had happened.

Sightings of the hooded figure, and of the disappearing group of children, are still regularly reported even to this day and no adequate explanation has ever been offered.

One theory is that ghosts need environmental energy to "feed" off of in order to manifest. The newly built pylon, with its tens of thousands of volts surging through, would have been like a huge beacon to them. The children were dancing around the pylon as it gave them a power that they'd needed for centuries thus finally allowing them to fully manifest.

Since the road opened there have been a disproportionate number of both fatal and serious

accidents. Between 1988 and 2002, when the road was improved, that five mile stretch of road averaged two deaths a year. All that extra investment only saw that figure drop so rather than a death every 6 months it was now seeing a death roughly every 9
months.

As well as the unusually high number of fatal accidents on the road there have also been countless near misses. Many of the drivers in question claim to have been swerving to avoid a hooded figure that had appeared suddenly in front of their vehicles before vanishing.

Who is this mysterious hooded figure? And what connection, if any, does he have to the disappearing children?

A popular local legend claims that the children died in a mining accident, a shaft collapsed causing a sinkhole beneath them, in which they fell and were lost forever. However the history of the area shows that there was no history of mining. However it does have a much more likely origin to offer.

Could the children be the ghosts of the passengers of a bus that crashed off of the original Pea Royd bridge back in the 1920s? The old bus tumbled down the steep hill sadly killing many of those on board.

Perhaps they're now a warning apparition, telling of the arrival of the hooded figure, whose sudden manifestation might even have been responsible for their own deaths?

There have been a couple of fatal accidents in the last decade where someone in the car had been on their phone at the time of the accident. Those on the other end of the line all have the same story to tell.

Typically the passenger that they're talking with will scream that there's a hooded man on the road, there will be a screech of brakes, and then the line goes dead.

The hooded figure is almost like some kind of Grim Reaper and he's one responsible for over a dozen deaths. Most ghost sightings are ultimately benign. But not this figure. He's out for blood any way he can get it.

As well as the children and that menacing hooded figure there's another ghost regularly seen around the bypass and he's become arguably the most well known. He's said to be a monk.

The Monk was said to appear in the middle of the road, on his knees as if deep in prayer, thus causing those who see him to swerve out the way to avoid him.

He's been seen hundreds of times but, unlike sightings of the hooded figure, sightings of the monk rarely have led to accidents.

One such sighting happened to a married couple,

who initially slowed down as they thought it was a person waiting to cross the road, only to realise that it was the monk. This time he was said to be hovering above the road surface and floating serenely across it. This sighting happened on New Year's Eve 1997.

Unlike the children and the hooded figure, who appear to be confined to the bypass, the monk has been spotted all throughout Stocksbridge.

A local bus driver and his friend had a run in with the monk whilst walking home one night. They felt the temperature around them drop colder and colder and described it as feeling like they had walked into a freezer. Stopping to wonder what was going on they noticed the figure of the monk was running through a field next to them, frantically flailing his arm, as if desperately trying to get their attention.

Initially assuming that they were the victims of a practical joke, they soon realised that what they were watching was something else entirely, as the figure vanished before reappearing instantly at the exact spot they had first spotted him and resuming his run. This repeated a half dozen times more before the two men, who were up until that point frozen in fear, managed to make a hasty retreat and fled back down the road.

Local legend says that he is supposedly the ghost of a Monk who worked on one of the Monastic Farms that were once spread throughout the area back in the middle ages. He was buried on unhallowed ground that was disturbed during the bypasses construction and his spirit has been wandering the area ever since looking for a final resting place.

All we know for sure is that something strange is going on around the Stocksbridge Bypass.

Something that has resulted in that five mile stretch of road having a fatality rate hundreds of times higher than the national average and that the ghosts there have been witnessed by thousands of people.

THE LIZARD'S OF RIVELIN VALLEY

Rivelin Valley, to the west of Sheffield, is a stunningly beautiful place.

Back in the 1800s work was carried out on the park that saw the construction of the current reservoirs. It was all part of a wider scheme to improve drinking water in that part of the city.

During the construction, conservationists got up in arms as they believed that the works would result in the loss of habitat of three rare species of lizards.

The first of which was the Running Askar. Said to resemble a wingless dragon, standing at just under two feet tall, it was a creature that looked like it had come straight out of a fairy tale. It was so named because it was said to run at great speeds making it almost impossible to catch.

The second was the Water Asker. This more closely resembled a very large newt and was said to be fully aquatic, having made its home in the shallow Rivelin River, from which the area took his name.

The last of the lizards was by far the most unusual of the three and that was the Flying Asker. This one was said to most closely resemble a wyvern, a kind of winged dragon, and it was also said to be the smallest of the three.

With a wingspan of just 6 inches, and a body length of just 3 inches, it was a dragon but in miniature. Its distinctive, mournful, cry was often said to be heard in the area.

Belief in the three species of lizard was so widespread that the council almost delayed construction on the scheme over their supposed presence.

It's worth noting that both the Water and Running Asker have not been sighted since. This does lend weight to the idea of it being a hoax. Perhaps a local landowner was worried that the park might have an impact on their view so concocted stories of the lizard?

However the small, wyvern-like, Winged Asker has been seen a handful of times since.

However it's the lizard's mournful cry that has been most widely reported. Said to resemble a haunting lament, the cry instils a deep sadness in all those who hear it.

Perhaps there really were once three unknown, and closely related, lizard species in that valley and the

ADRIAN FINNEY

Winged Asker now sings of their loss?

THE FLOATING FEET OF ANGEL STREET

Scholfield's Department Store was a once much loved shop in the centre of town that was also home to a strange, recurring, manifestation in both the store's stockroom and in its boiler room.

That manifestation? A pair of feet, only visible to just above the ankle, and that would walk and dance around whilst actually floating around 4 feet above the ground.

The feet were first sighted when workers were installing the store's heating system. Hearing footsteps the two workmen turned a corner and face to foot with the floating feet as they were walking around. They fled in fear although no one at the time took their sighting seriously.

After the store had been open for a few months the feet were back, only this time they were said to be dancing around the stockroom, and the worker who saw them was memorised. To her? It was a most wonderful sight.

Over the next few years the feet were seen so often that the staff developed an almost blaise attitude towards them.

By the 1990s business wasn't doing so well and Sheffield lost one of its much loved institutions when Schofields closed its doors for good.

Opening in its place was an Argos and, despite many internal changes, the feet came back, happily performing and dancing for all those willing to watch.

In 2021 Argos moved out which once again left the former Schofield's store empty.

Looking into the site's history the store was built on what was once a warehouse for the Royal Windsor China company. And throughout that warehouse's existence there were sightings of the same feet. Only back then they were never said to float. They'd walk around at ground level.

We can therefore presume that the feet are still adhering to the floor level of the original building.

There was a legend that a worker, daydreaming of one day dancing on the stage, tripped and fell to their death.

Do the feet belong to that worker? Finally finding the limelight from the other side?

And will the workers of whatever opens next in that

building once again see the feet? Only time will tell. Perhaps one day someone might be quick with their phone and capture some fabulous footage of the fantastical floating feet of Angel Street.

THE RED CLOUD OF WOODTHORPE

In February 2017 panicked residents in the Woodthorpe area of Sheffield were convinced that there was a house fire.

Looking out they could see a red cloud, hanging low over a nearby rooftop, so they decided to call the fire brigade. However before they had the chance to dial 999 the cloud lifted itself up to an altitude of around 100ft and began hovering slowly around the area.

Multi coloured beams started shooting out of the object, as though it was scanning for something, mostly green, blue, and pink.

After fifteen minutes or so the cloud, or whatever it was, headed off towards Arbourthorne.

In total around a dozen people witnessed the object. People attempted to take footage of the cloud but found that every time they aimed their phones at the object their photo sensors failed.

Oddly enough it wasn't the first time that such an

object had been seen in the skies over Sheffield.

Back in 1731 a glowing red "devils cloud" was seen that "belched rainbows."

Could this have been the same object witnessed centuries apart? That would make it a repeat visitor to the area. If so, it begs the question: what does it want? And when will it return?

THE HOUND OF HILLSBOROUGH

It was the late 1960s and it was a quiet night in Hillsborough. Or at least that's what the Police Constable on duty thought.

Then a call came in. There was apparently a large dog running amok along Taplin Road.

The Constable decided it would be worth investigating. It could be a much loved family pet that had bolted. Or perhaps it was a public danger? Either way, he thought, this was police business.

In just a few short minutes he arrived on the scene. There were terrified residents shouting out of their windows telling him to beware the Hellhound.

Bemused, he wondered to himself just how big was this dog meant to be, to have the street in such uproar?

It was then that he heard it.

A low, deep, growl coming from behind him. He spun round and saw nothing. The growl began again so he once again spun round and this time he saw the dog. It was about 100 yards away from him and it was in a low, defensive, position.

He slowly, but confidently, walked towards the dog. He remembered from his training that the secret to securing a dog was confidence.

When he got within 20 yards of the dog it reared up as though ready to pounce.

Despite being startled the policeman held his ground. Then the dog lept towards him, teeth bared, in an apparent attack.

The policeman had just enough time to close his eyes and put his hands up in a defensive posture. He waited for the inevitable pain a bite from this huge dog would bring but that pain never arrived.

He warily opened an eye and looked around. There was no dog. He knew it had pounced towards him. And he knew that should have been that.

He was confused. Had the dog missed and scarpered? It must have. What other explanation was there?

Then the growl was back. This time louder than ever and he felt a deep fear in his stomach.

Before he had the chance to react the dog pounced at him again. But, much to his surprise, the dog lept straight *through* him!

He looked around and saw no dog. He did, however, strongly smell brimstone.

What on Earth had happened? He looked up at the houses and they'd all closed their windows and drew the curtains.

Fine, he thought, if Taplin Road wanted to pretend this had never happened? Then that was more than alright by him.

He'd put it down as a false alarm back at the station. He didn't have the time to be chasing ghostly dogs.

Twenty years later, when the PC was nearing retirement, a young officer came to him for advice about a funny dog he'd seen on Taplin Road, one that had apparently disappeared in a puff of smoke.

The older officer, rather than laugh, told him they'd both go for a stiff drink when they finished their shift as he had a story to tell.

THE OLD QUEEN'S HEAD

The Old Queen's Head pub is the oldest surviving domestic building in Sheffield. It was first mentioned back in a 1582 census of the area but is likely much older.

It's also home to a few of Sheffield's most jovial ghosts.

Drinkers from the 17th century all the way up to the present day have described near identical encounters.

They'd happily be sat with their pint, having a good time, when it would feel like time was slowing down. Some have described it as like wading through treacle. Whilst this was happening the sounds of the busy pub began to fade away with many saying it sounded like they had found themselves under water.

It's then that they notice him. An old man, with a warm and friendly face, leaning against the stone fireplace. He is then always said to raise his jug of beer up in greeting to whoever sees him.

Those who have witnessed him describe it as like suddenly seeing an old, long lost, friend.

They then blink and it's like the bubble they were in breaks. Time once again flows as normal and the typical sounds of a busy pub rush back in.

Just like that the ghost's manifestation is over.

Who is he? We don't know. But local legend says he is the ghost of the pub's very first landlord keeping an eye on his pub, and its punters, from beyond the grave.

He's not the only otherworldly visitor to the pub. One of the others is often heard, but never seen, in the pub's cellar.

Back when the pub was originally constructed it had a well in the cellar. This was bricked off back in the 17th century as it had dried up.

However on quiet nights footsteps and whispering can be heard coming from behind the bricked up wall.

Is there a dark secret down there waiting to be unearthed? Only time will tell.

VICKERS CORRIDOR - NORTHERN GENERAL HOSPITAL

It's a widely held belief that most hospitals are haunted. Any place that sees the full range of the human conditions, from birth to death, is likely to be.

But I think it's fair to say that Sheffield's Northern General Hospital is more haunted than most. In fact it has enough ghost stories to fill several books all on its own. The tale I've chosen to tell is that of one the hospital's most malevolent spirits.

Back in 2003 a young nurse was catching up on a little bit of sleep whilst working a double shift. She was in the staff room, then located on the Vickers Corridor, and awoke with a shock.

Someone had her pinned down and a huge hand was choking her. As her eyes came into focus she could see it was a fellow nurse. But one in a very old matron's uniform. It was perhaps a century old?

She struggled and struggled to break free. The lights flickered and the towering figure of the matron simply blinked out of existence. Returning to the ward to continue her shift she was ready to dismiss her experience as a bad dream.

When she got to the ward, however, she found that was not the case. The ward sister grabbed her and asked was she okay? What had happened? Did she need the police calling? Because on the young nurse's neck she could see the angry red outline of the hand that had been choking her.

She sent the nurse over to the hospital's A&E department to be given the once over. The doctor there took one look at her neck, that angry red hand print, and said softly "Vickers Corridor Staffroom?"

Shocked, the young nurse nodded. The Doctor then told her that back when she was on her final placement in the hospital she too had slept in that staffroom and that she too had been attacked by the angry ghost matron.

And that in the 15 years she'd been working in A&E she'd met over 3 dozen hospital staff all with the same red hand print.

Who this matron is? We don't know.

But that part of the hospital dates from the late 1800s and was originally built as a workhouse. So perhaps she's the spirit of one of the workhouse matrons and she is intent on punishing anyone she sees as slacking off.

The young nurse returned to work to finish her shift but she never again slept in that staffroom.

THE SHEFFIELD INCIDENT

It was just before 10pm on the 24th March 1997. In the Peak District, just outside of Sheffield, something was about to happen. But what exactly that something was is still hotly debated even to this day.

It began with a multitude of 999 calls all describing a low flying aircraft that had been seen heading over the hills and then there was a bright flash and the sound of a loud explosion.

South Yorkshire and Derbyshire Police began a combined operation as they feared that they were dealing with a downed aircraft. The fire service and specialist mountain rescue units were all called in as was a police helicopter.

As more and more calls came in, a call was made, and the local hospitals put on high alert. The police were so certain, based on the sheer volume of calls coming, that there had been a plane crash. This was standard procedure in case there were any survivors.

The police contacted Air Traffic Control and the RAF only to be told that they had no record of any aircraft in the area at that time, downed, or otherwise.

However, at the Police's insistence, the RAF agreed to help with the search and sent a couple of Sea King Search and Rescue helicopters to assist. With calls still coming in from witnesses spread all across North East Sheffield and the Peak District there was a real sense of urgency and a drive to find whatever it was that had come down.

A total of 40 square miles were searched that night but supposedly nothing was found.

The following morning the police set up a specific hotline for members of the public to report anything unusual that they might have seen in the skies the night before.

The hotline crashed, twice, under the weight of the calls. No one was expecting as many calls that they had let alone the fact that they all were telling the same story.

All the sightings told of a strange looking, low flying, triangular object along with military jets that were described as being in hot pursuit.

At the grounds of Sheffield FC, in Dronfield, a football match was underway on the night in question. About five minutes before the final whistle the ground shook as two jets thundered past low overhead. The players, along with the crowd of around 150 people, all stopped and looked up. It was then that they spotted the triangular object, which they described as being similar in size to a commercial jetliner and much bigger than the military jets, fly directly overhead.

Unlike the loud roar of the jets this object was emitting a low pulsing hum similar to that of an electrical transformer. After the object had flown overhead two more jets sped by clearly in hot pursuit. They didn't know what it was that they had seen but they all knew it was definitely something out of the ordinary.

A retired RAF pilot, who was in the crowd watching his son play, assumed that what they were witnessing was a secret test aircraft and wondered to himself who exactly authorised a flight that would take it over a built up area.

This all occurred less than 7 minutes before the alleged crash happened. It's worth noting that the distance from Dronfield to Howden Reservoir could easily have been covered by the slow moving triangular object in half that time and could have been covered in less than 90 seconds if the pursuing jets had decided to throttle up.

Sightings were coming in from across the region. The triangular object looked to have made land over Lincolnshire then proceeded to travel in roughly a straight line to Dronfield before arching sharply

North.

It appears that it was the skies above Dronfield where the pursuing jets made contact with the object and the chase began. The police were baffled.

It should be pointed out that the night in question was a clear but cold night and that there were thousands of people outside stargazing which was a fairly unusual occurrence. This was because the famed Hale Bopp comet was due to go past at about 10:30pm so lots of people were out hoping to catch a glimpse.

Officially we know that RAF had set up a ten mile exclusion zone centred on Howden Reservoir and that this was in place until mid afternoon on the 25th March 1997. This was where the witnesses had all placed the alleged crash so because of this it became the centre of their search. Officially this was the RAFs only involvement in the incident. A stance that would eventually be contradicted in Parliament.

Various theories began to circulate, ranging from it being a light aircraft crashing that had been involved in an illegal drugs drop, to a ghost plane sighting like the one that is said to appear in the skies above Owler Bar.

However one of the more persuasive theories, given the volume of eye witness statements, was that a squadron of RAF Tornados were in pursuit of an

Unidentified Flying Object across the U.K. The chase took them from the skies above the North Sea to the skies above the Peak District. It's there where one of two things might have happened.

Either one of the Tornados crashed or the Tornados managed to successfully bring down the UFO that they were chasing.

Whatever it was that crashed, Tornado or UFO, it was said to have crashed into the remote Howden Reservoir. A location on the reservoir's shore was the spot where the RAFs hastily set up 10 mile exclusion zone was centred. Rather than being the centre of a fruitless search, as was the official version of events, instead it was to facilitate the recovery of whatever it was that had been downed in secrecy as well as allowing them the time to remove any evidence that a crash had taken place.

It's worth noting that it wasn't just the Sea King search and rescue helicopters that were spotted in the skies that night. Three Chinooks, with their distinctive twin rotor blades, were also said to have landed next to the reservoir in the early hours of the 25th before leaving the area around midday. A couple of sightings even allege the Chinooks were carrying something heavy suspended below them when they left.

Despite all this the police's official response was:

'No explanation was ever found and we remain open-

minded about what was behind the sightings.'

That could easily have been that for the incident. However local residents were so sure of what it was that they had seen, and so angered by what they felt was an obvious cover up from the police and the government, they petitioned their MPs and the government for a response.

On the 23rd of March 1998, almost a full year after the incident took place, it was brought up in the House of Commons by Helen Jackson, the then MP for Sheffield Hillsborough, as Howden Reservoir was located within her constituency.

A week later, on the 30th of March 1998, the Ministry of Defence finally responded.

The MOD finally admitted that there was indeed a low flying military exercise taking place over Northern England on the night in question. A fact that fully contradicted the RAF, who had spent the previous year repeating their official stance that no such exercise had taken place, and the Civil Aviation Authority who also claimed that no planes were operating in the area that night.

It was apparently a covert low altitude exercise that involved both Tornado and Jaguar jets. It's worth noting that the Jaguar was a delta wing aircraft, giving it something of a triangular shape when viewed from below.

Nothing was said to have crashed. But the MOD

had an explanation on hand as to the cause of the flashes and the explosion. The flashes were from flares set off by hikers and the explosion's sound would have actually been a bolide meteor entering the atmosphere as it would have caused a supersonic boom.

The problem with the MODs new version of events was that there wasn't just the one sonic boom that night. There were two. The first one took place at 21.52 and the second happened fourteen minutes later at 22.06.

We know this because of the National Geological Survey. One of their key roles is to monitor the United Kingdom for such events and in a typical year they detect around 300 sonic booms. They have monitoring stations spread across the whole country and they are used to triangulate the locations of unexplained sonic booms. The data is compiled and processed by the University of Edinburgh.

Three tracking stations picked up both sonic booms on the night in question and both occurred in the vicinity of Howden Reservoir.

They refused to be drawn in on a cause of the sonic booms but they did state that they were most likely to have been caused by one of two things. They were either from an aircraft breaking the sound barrier or they were space debris entering and then burning up in the atmosphere.

When asked later they also acknowledged that an aircraft, such as a Tornado, crashing into a body of water such as Howden Reservoir would also have generated a sound the recording equipment would have registered as a sonic boom.

Despite the MOD finally admitting that there were indeed aircraft in the area that night, the RAF have maintained their denial, repeatedly stating that they had no aircraft in the area at the time, and the CAA said that their RADAR records were only kept for a year which meant that they were unable to offer any further help. If the question had been raised in Parliament just a week or two earlier however? Then the CAA would still have had records for the time frame in question.

As for the RAF? They went on to say that it is against the law to break the sound barrier over land in the UK and that they had no record of any sonic booms caused by RAF or NATO airforce ally aircraft on the night in question.

The RAF also said that their exclusion zone was imposed solely in response to a request from the police following those initial 999 calls and that this was routine in such circumstances.

So we're left with a mystery. The MOD confirmed that there were indeed military jets flying over the Peak District that night, but the RAF have repeatedly said that they didn't belong to them nor were they the jets of any other NATO ally's Air Force, so that begs the question whose jets were they? And what were they chasing to warrant the use of supersonic flight so close to a built up area?

Of course this is all assuming that any of this did actually happen.

By this point the closest thing offered to an "official" explanation is that several things happened that night all at the same time. That there was an unknown light aircraft flying low overhead, which coincided with someone setting a flare off to explain away the flash, and both of these events also coincided precisely with two pieces of space junk re-entering the atmosphere.

Which is an awful lot of coincidences and, as explanations go, is awfully convoluted.

A more likely explanation would be to admit that something unusual did indeed happen in the skies that night. And that either the RAF are actively lying about their involvement or, perhaps more likely, that their use of the term "airforce" is the key to understanding what might have actually happened. It's an awfully specific term.

What if an object was picked up flying over the North Sea but it wasn't RAF jets that were scrambled that night. What if, instead, it was jets from the Fleet Air Arm? They are as well equipped as the RAF, having some of the best fighter and reconnaissance aircraft in existence, but crucially they're operated under the umbrella of The Royal Navy NOT The Royal Air Force.

The jets, spotting the unusual flying triangle, were given authorization to pursue. Based on the hundreds, if not thousands, of eyewitness reports we have we can even put something of a timeline to the events of March 24th 1997.

At some point after 9pm the triangle was picked up heading towards the U.K. mainland from out over the North Sea. Shortly after this a squadron of interceptor jets, most likely Tornadoes, were scrambled to investigate the object. A pursuit began and, at about 9:35pm, the pursuit reached the mainland around Boston, Lincolnshire. From there the triangle and the jets travelled roughly North West for ten minutes when, at 9:45pm, they were sighted in the skies above Dronfield. Here the object turned sharply North which brought it over large parts of Sheffield thus causing that huge wave of sightings.

At 9:52pm one of the pursuing jets, most likely a Tornado given the witnesses reports, crashed into Howden Reservoir. The noise from this would account for the first of the recorded sonic booms.

Multiple reports from around High Bradfield, Stocksbridge, Holmfirth, and as far away as Castleford and Hathersage all reported hearing the crash as well as seeing the military jets racing back and forth overhead.

Tabulating the reports it appears that the crash happened during a low level pursuit that took place confined within a rough triangle, with the points being at Tideswell in the south, Holmfirth to the north, and Stocksbridge in the east. From the accounts given the Tornadoes, despite being designed specifically for low altitude dog fights, would still have been flying close to their stall speed to try and match the slow moving triangle.

Perhaps it was this, stalling, that caused the aircraft to crash?

At 10:06pm we know for a fact that the second sonic boom happened. This, we can hypothesise, was the triangular object leaving the area at supersonic, or possibly even hypersonic, speeds following a 14 minute low altitude back and forth between the triangle and the Tornadoes.

After this second sonic boom the jets, that had until that point been in hot pursuit, broke off and returned to base. After 10:06pm we had no further sightings from over the Peak District.

However there were further sightings of the jets. At 10:08pm they flew over Parsons Cross and at 10:09pm they were spotted over Wincobank. Given that the sight of military jets is a fairly unusual one in the skies above the UK, and thanks to the amount of people looking up waiting for the Hale Bopp comet, we can trace them all the way back to RAF Conisby. It was here where they landed just before half past ten.

At 11:05pm a motorist on the A57, about 6 miles away from the alleged crash site, spotted a man standing at the side of the road. He pulled over to offer him a lift, as it was very unusual and dangerous to see any pedestrians on that stretch of road, especially at that time of night. The man kindly refused the offer and told him that it was okay, he had a lift coming. Just forget him. He'd be fine.

The driver, who had rolled his windows down to speak with the man, noted that he smelt strongly of jet fuel. Sensing something was off, the driver carried on his journey. Within minutes he spotted several police cars and an ambulance heading at speed in the direction he had seen the man. He looked down over the valley beneath him and also spotted the Sea King helicopters with their search beams shining brightly.

A short while later he passed through a police roadblock. The PC asked him had he seen the crash? Then a plain suited man walked up explaining that there was no crash. It was a false alarm. Just forget he'd seen anything. But he didn't forget. He reported his sighting via the police hotline the following morning but nothing ever came of it.

At least, based on this eyewitness account, we can

assume that the pilot managed to safely eject from the downed aircraft.

What we are left with then is a whole lot of evidence, a multitude of eye witnesses, for an incident that never officially happened.

Of the many questions we are left with perhaps the most obvious is where did the flying triangle come from? One rumour is that it was a secret Russian aircraft investigating and pushing the UKs air defences. These incursions are fairly commonplace for conventional fighter jets. It's a constant cat and mouse game that has been going on since the Cold War.

However sending a top secret aircraft, that is still clearly classified to this day, would have been seen as an act of war. It's also worth pointing out that the characteristics of the triangle are very similar to the often rumoured US secret stealth plane codenamed Project Aurora. That, too, is said to be a hypersonic triangular craft. Could Russia have built their own version? And have been testing it in U.K. airspace?

There are several problems with the Russia explanation.

Firstly, should the triangular craft have been theirs and then been shot down or crashed, it would have led to a diplomatic incident or possibly even a war. Russia can be very bold in their actions but would they have risked a war just for a flight test? It's unlikely but it can't be ruled out.

Another issue is that all of the hypersonic aircraft we have developed, such as the SR71 Blackbird, have very high stall speeds and are built to be flown at high altitudes. We currently don't have the technology to engineer an aircraft that behaved in the manner that the triangle did.

There is a version of the Russian origin tale that claims it was the triangle that crashed into the reservoir that night. But fearing war both our government and the Russian government hastily covered the whole incident up. If we pretend it didn't happen? Then it didn't happen.

The problem with that theory is that the presumed pilot, the man who smelt of jet fuel, had a British accent not a Russian one. Of course this doesn't rule out it being a Russian craft but it does make it somewhat unlikely.

Discounting the Russians as the ones operating the triangle we are left with an altogether more out there explanation. What if the triangle was extra terrestrial in its origin? Perhaps it was a reconnaissance ship, given its large size, that found itself on the wrong side of the Royal Navy?

How many Boeing 747 sized aircrafts can match RAF Tornado jets in a low altitude pursuit in terms of both speed and manoeuvrability? None that come from here that's for sure.

It's an out there idea. But it's no less likely than the mystery craft being Russian in origin or it being a particularly well witnessed spectral ghost plane sighting.

News on the incident went quiet until, in 2010, an amateur metal detectorist searching around Howden Reservoir made an interesting discovery. He found a handful of titanium fan blades, along with a few other pieces, all of which had most likely come from a jet engine. Some of the blades even showed signs of fire and impact damage. They were buried deep so could they have been missed in the hasty initial cover up?

A couple of the fan blades still had their manufacturing numbers legible on them. However, after much investigation, their maker could never be identified. Given that part numbers are a part of the public record this was highly unusual.

One thing we do know is that they would have been the right size to have been from a Tornado jet. Could this be the much needed evidence to prove that, back in 1997, an aircraft did indeed crash into Howden Reservoir? It would appear so.

This is a frustrating incident. We have so much evidence, from eye witness reports to the sonic booms being officially recorded, we have the MOD denying and then, over a year later, acknowledging that there were planes in the sky that night, but despite all of this we are no closer to finding out what truly happened that night.

We can say with certainty that something strange took place in the skies over the Peak District that night.

We can say with relative certainty that an aircraft was downed, crashing into Howden Reservoir, but beyond that?

We simply don't know.

A GHOST ON FARGATE

The WH Smith's store on Fargate, Sheffield, spent much of 2018 closed for business due to emergency repairs. The iconic early 19th century exterior may remain but inside it is now a whole new store.

Severe structural issues were found with the 3rd floor and the roof and they meant that the entire building was at risk of collapse. If the building was to stand for a further 200 years something had to be done. This resulted in the third floor being essentially rebuilt as was the roof.

It's now a very modern building behind, and holding up, that classic facade.

However, like many similar old buildings that face such structural work, the repairs appear to have awoken a few long dormant spirits.

Ted, not his real name, was working for the firm who were contracted with renovating the interior of the store itself.

He'd come into work early that day and he was well on his way with installing some new neon light fixtures. It was then that he noticed a figure walking through the shop.

The doors should have been locked, and more so than that there was a fence around the frontage, so it should have just been him in that day. He checked his watch and saw that his colleague wasn't due in for another hour.

He looked over at the figure. It was that of an older gentleman, dressed in a very old fashioned way Ted thought, and he was carrying a white cane. The white cane… That caused a memory to come forward. Oh!

Ted quickly realised with a jolt exactly what that meant.

He had a blind man, walking around the very much unfinished store, where there were live wires dangling from the ceiling.

Ted shouted out to the man but he didn't appear to hear him. So he leapt from his ladder and that's when he realised he was caught up in the wiring of the sign he was installing. The whole piece of newly installed signage, two days' work for poor Ted, came down with a clatter.

Ted looked at the mess around him and swore. It was then he noticed that the old man wasn't there anymore. Ted was located by the door. The other doors were all locked. So where had he gone?

Blind men don't just disappear into the ether do

they? Ted was certain he'd seen the man.

It was then that Ted's colleague walked in. He was not impressed by the mess, but he listened carefully to what Ted said he saw, and it is safe to say he was not convinced that Ted had seen anything out of the ordinary at all.

Ted finished off the job at WH Smith's but he never again saw the figure. He did, however, end up putting up with ridicule from a few of his work mates over his supposed ghost sighting. It's this fear of ridicule which is why we aren't using his real name here. It's also a huge barrier that prevents a great deal of ghost sightings from ever being reported.

A few weeks later Ted received a call from one of the workers at WH Smith's. The store was being restocked ready for its grand reopening and the employee cautiously asked him *"Are you the man who saw the ghost?"*

Before he had chance to reply he heard *"I've seen him too..."*

There were a few details, such as the white cane and the gentleman's somewhat oversized flat cap, that Ted had left out of his story. But hearing these details from someone else confirmed to him that he hadn't been mistaken. If someone else has seen it too then it was, undeniably, real.

During the first 6 months after the store reopened

the figure was sighted at least a half dozen more times. He was always seen within the first hour of the store opening and always said to disappear in the blink of an eye.

After that the sightings settled down and the figure hasn't been seen since.

That being said, if you saw a blind man walking around a shop would you give him a second look?

It's possible, if not probable, that he's still there to this day. It's just that those witnessing his ghost haven't reallsed just how extraordinary the sight before them truly is. He's a ghost that, at a glance at least, appears part of the mundane everyday world around us.

Unfortunately a look into the building's history hasn't given us any clues as to the identity of the blind man.

However it's possible he was working on the site during the building's initial construction and died as the result of an accident.

During the Victorian era it was expected that those who were blind would learn skills suitable for "useful toil," in one of a selected list of trades, and this was a view that carried on until relatively recently. "Useful toil" being a lovely Victorian era euphemism for paying their own way.

One of these "blind trades" was rope making. That

was a very useful, and highly in demand, skill to have on a construction site in an era before cranes and modern machinery.

Could he have been mending a frayed piece of rope before unwittingly losing his life in an accident? We can't say for sure.

But it appears that his spirit had been resting peacefully for over a century. It was only the severe structural renovations, and the disruption they caused, that led to his spirit once again walking around that building in Fargate.

And who knows, next time you're buying a paper in WH Smith's, you too might just catch a glimpse of his ghost.

GABRIEL'S HOUNDS

We began this book with a tale of the Black Dog of Bunting Nook so it is fitting that we end with the story of another ghostly dog sighting.

Stannington, to the west of Sheffield, is the region's oldest inhabited area. Archeologists have found evidence of human settlements here dating as far back as the Bronze Age.

From the Middle Ages, right up to the most recent sighting in the early 1990s, it's also been home to a pack of ghostly hounds, known as Gabriel's Hounds.

Most dogs of folklore are said to resemble that of the Black Dog of Bunting Nook. Huge monstrous things, with glowing red eyes, but definitely canine in appearance.

Gabriel's Hounds are said to have an altogether stranger appearance. They're the size of a Labrador and look like a typical dog from the neck backwards. However they don't have the head of a dog. Instead they are said to have the head of a person. More specifically? The head of a small child. They also have the ability to fly in packs.

They are rarely seen, but their howls are often heard, and hearing one is said to mean that there is going to be a death in the area.

However, when they're seen, that's when death is truly close by. They are said to land on the roofs of houses where someone is about to die and begin their howl. The sight of them is said to bring a shiver to your very soul.

Back in the 17th century it was said that Gabriel's Hounds were actually the souls of unbaptised children. No one is even sure where their name originates from.

Perhaps they are still there, prowling the skies above Stannington ready to announce imminent deaths, they're just no longer heard.

Since their last sightings we all are now walking along, oblivious, looking down at our phones, headphones firmly in, so they go by unnoticed.

But they're there. Always there. Always watching. And if we fear for a loved one in that area perhaps we had best keep an ear out for their distinctive howl.

THE PHANTOM PATROLMAN

TAKEN FROM STRANGE NOTTINGHAM (AVAILABLE NOW)

It was 2002 and the weather was, in a word, atrocious. Gary and his family were heading out of Nottingham towards Derby on the A52 when they heard a loud bang. They'd suffered a blown tire. Cursing to himself, but thankful he'd a mobile, he rang the AA for assistance.

It was the early hours and the road was unusually quiet that stormy night. After about ten minutes one of Gary's children noticed a lone headlight heading towards them. A motorbike out in this weather?

As the motorbike drew level with the car the family spotted the familiar logo of the AA emblazoned on its funny looking sidecar. Gary vaguely remembered he had a toy AA motorbike and sidecar that had been passed down to him from his father.

Lowering his window he now clearly saw that this was no ordinary AA man. He was on a very old motorbike that must have dated back to at least the 1930s.

The patrolman saluted Gary as he passed him. Then, for the briefest of seconds, the rain stopped and the wind ceased. In that moment of calm they saw the motorcycle speed away and then simply vanish. Over the course of just a few seconds it faded to nothing and all that could be seen of it was the red glow of its rear light. Once that too had vanished the calmness ended and the wind and rain returned with a vengeance.

Gary relayed his story to the AA man who finally arrived, in his van, about half an hour later. The man smiled. He'd heard of this phantom patrolman a great many times on this particular stretch of road.

Apparently one November in 1934 a Patrolman was racing along in bad weather. A tree had blown down directly in front of him, that had caused him to lose control, and he had died in the ensuing crash.

But ever since then, on dark and stormy nights, he'd be seen completing his patrol and on occasion, like with Gary and his family, offering a little comfort and reassurance that help was on its way.

AFTERWORD

I would like to thank you all for reading this book. The strange tales you've just read merely scratch the surface of the weirdness our steel city contains.

Perhaps you have had an encounter with one of the spirits within and this book has given you peace of mind. And as much as it might be hard to process, you really did see what you think you saw, and others have seen it too.

Or perhaps you half remember something in the skies overhead and now you know that you were not alone in what you saw.

Stories of the strange and of the weird have fascinated us for centuries. There is something inside all of us that loves a story that can not be easily explained. When there are multiple witnesses or if it's a sighting that is said to repeat? Even better.

It means we too might have a chance, however small, to get a glimpse at what is really out there.

And with that we might find those deeper answers humanity has spent its existence searching for.

It was only a few hundred years ago when Gorillas were considered as mystical as the Yeti and the Loch Ness Monster. We've had reliable flight for a little over a century.

So who knows what we may discover in the next hundred years? If there's one thing, above all else, I'd like you to take from this book it's curiosity.

We live in a strange and exciting world.

Explore it.

If you would like to contact me, perhaps with a story of your own, or to discuss something in this book I would love to hear from you.

My email is:

strangebritainofficial@gmail.com

And you can find and message me under the name "Strange Britain" on both Facebook and Instagram.

Printed in Great Britain
by Amazon